SPELLCASTER'S
LOGBOOK

AN INTERACTIVE GUIDE TO MAKING MAGIC

BY SARAH LONGSTRETH

Peter Pauper Press, Inc.

WHITE PLAINS, NEW YORK

PETER PAUPER PRESS
Fine Books and Gifts Since 1928

Our Company

In 1928, at the age of twenty-two, Peter Beilenson began printing books on a small press in the basement of his parents' home in Larchmont, New York. Peter—and later, his wife, Edna—sought to create fine books that sold at "prices even a pauper could afford."

Today, still family owned and operated, Peter Pauper Press continues to honor our founders' legacy—and our customers' expectations—of beauty, quality, and value.

For Sarah Carter, with fond gratitude for your wisdom and wit

Special thanks to Rowan Crane, Michelle Houslanger, and Emma Watson

Cover designed by Heather Zschock
Interior designed by Margaret Rubiano

Copyright © 2022 Peter Pauper Press, Inc.
202 Mamaroneck Avenue
White Plains, NY 10601 USA
All rights reserved
ISBN 978-1-4413-3809-9
Printed in China

Published in the United Kingdom and Europe by
Peter Pauper Press, Inc. c/o White Pebble International
Unit 2, Plot 11 Terminus Road
Chichester, West Sussex PO19 8TX, UK
7 6 5 4 3 2 1

Visit us at www.peterpauper.com

CONTENTS

WELCOME

DO YOU BELIEVE IN MAGIC? WHATEVER YOU CALL IT, you probably do. No matter what we learn about the world, people are made for magical thinking. When we knock on wood for good luck, cheer for our favorite team to win, or even make a cup of tea to wake up or calm down, we're putting energy toward what we want to happen, hoping to make it real. Drawing the right card at the perfect time, hearing your song on the radio just when you need it, finding an amazing parking spot—it can feel, in some small way, as if it's all because of you. What if you could take luck in your own hands, and turn your wishes into reality?

Making magic means you'll use your mind to change the world. Maybe you want to seize success, or help a friend, or send something wicked away. There's no one-size-fits-all spellbook for that—because there isn't one right way to be a witch. In this book, you'll create spells unique to you and your desires.

Take a crash course in the craft of magic with the next few pages. Just like making a recipe, growing a garden, or writing a story, there are steps you can practice and skills you can learn. Use this interactive guide to record your spells and see what works for you.

You've always had the power. You just need to learn it for yourself.

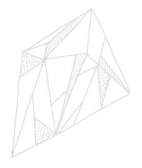

SPELL COMPONENTS

Combine your thoughts, words, actions, and materials, and you've got a spell. To start, you'll need this book, plus any other reading you'd like to consult. You'll build each spell based on an intention: an ideal outcome you want to bring into the world.

Then you'll gather your materials. There's a reason witches are so often pictured stirring potions in a kitchen full of strange plants and glowing jars. Materials matter—without something physical to anchor it, a spell lives only in your mind. Common items like candles, herbs, oils, and crystals can amplify all kinds of spells. You can find a quick guide to the basics in the back of this book.

You'll also need to choose a place to cast your spell. People who practice witchcraft often use an altar: a table, platform, or a flat stone decorated with magical materials and symbols of the season. Altars offer you a dedicated space to focus and practice your craft. If you make one, feel free to give it your own personal creative touch. Some witches opt not to use altars at all. Your kitchen, a corner of your bedroom, or a favorite tree work just as well.

When you're ready, do your ritual. Take an action, as simple or complicated as you like. Say, sing, or just think a few words about what you want to happen. Write it all down in this book, according to the steps on page 10. Over time, you'll see what manifests and learn more about your power.

SPELL CONDITIONS

Your willpower, goals, and space are all essential to spellcasting. Connecting with nature and the world around you can make a big difference too. A few things to keep in mind:

THE MOON

Life moves in cycles, just as the moon moves from new to full and back again. By paying attention to these patterns, you can find strength and consistency even in the midst of constant change. Each phase of the lunar cycle brings different energy that you can use to amplify your spells.

New: A blank slate with infinite potential. Use this time to welcome new beginnings, set new goals, find peace, and seek improvement.

Waxing: Boost your energy for expansion and growth. Try spells to strengthen creativity, courage, relationships, and success.

Full: Feel the power, and make your most ambitious intentions succeed. Supercharge your magical materials for the month to come by letting them soak in full moonlight.

Waning: Shrink and send away the negativity in your life. Write spells to say goodbye to anything you're done with and protect your light.

THE ELEMENTS

Five elements form the basis of magic: **fire**, for passion and willpower; **water**, for emotions and adaptability; **air**, for thought and freedom; **earth**, for stability and health; and **spirit**, a universal essence that unites all things. Call on the elements when you need a boost.

AS ABOVE, SO BELOW...

THE CALENDAR

Much like the moon, you can look to the seasons to inspire your spellcasting. The changing seasons strengthen different aspects of magical energy throughout the year. Eight holidays, or Sabbats, mark the beginnings of each season and notable dates in the middle. Use each season's themes to your advantage when you consider your intentions for a spell.

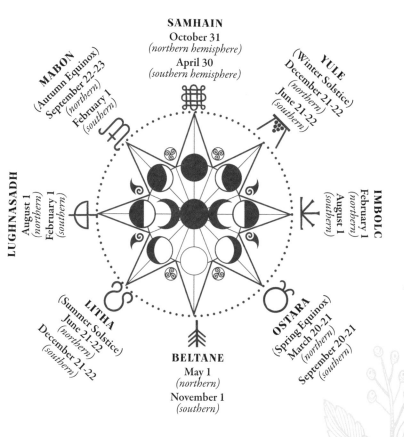

SAMHAIN
October 31
(northern hemisphere)
April 30
(southern hemisphere)

YULE
(Winter Solstice)
December 21-22
(northern)
June 21-22
(southern)

MABON
(Autumn Equinox)
September 22-23
(northern)
February 1
(southern)

LUGHNASADH
August 1
(northern)
February 1
(southern)

IMBOLC
February 1
(northern)
August 1
(southern)

LITHA
(Summer Solstice)
June 21-22
(northern)
December 21-22
(southern)

BELTANE
May 1
(northern)
November 1
(southern)

OSTARA
(Spring Equinox)
March 20-21
(northern)
September 20-21
(southern)

Samhain, best known in mainstream culture for its overlap with Halloween, is a night when the boundary blurs between the worlds of the living and dead. It's the best time to reach out and connect with those you've lost, honor their memories, and feel the ways their presence lingers in your life. Samhain also marks the beginning of the new year in some traditions, so go all out and get spooky with it. Who will you become when anything is possible?

Yule, the winter solstice, is the shortest day and longest night of the year. Look for the light and warmth of community, even in the darkest times, and you'll tap into the magic of this season. What does it mean to make a home? What new hopes can you nurture?

Imbolc is when the world reawakens from winter and takes its first step toward spring. The sun's return brings more energy for spells involving creativity or love. What you contemplate and cultivate now will blossom. What's sleeping inside you? Nudge it and see what awakens.

Ostara is the spring equinox, a day and night of equal length. With a balanced perspective, you can take care of anything—projects, plants, and people. Clean out the clutter in your space (and in your head). Look for ways to appreciate nature and make new starts. What refreshes you? Let it flourish.

Beltane, widely known as May Day, celebrates spring's big bloom and the coming of summer. Spells for love and fertility are at their strongest, and the good things in life are on full display. What are your passions? When's the last time you cut loose and danced? Now's the time to bring a burst of energy to everything you do.

Litha, the summer solstice, is the longest day in a season of warm, fleeting nights. Bright sunlight burns away bad energies and lights up the natural world. Fire magic is particularly strong on Litha night, so build a campfire or light a candle, make a wish, and mean it. Like all living things, you need light to grow. What powers your spirit? What can you will into being?

Lughnasadh, or **Lammas**, begins summer's tilt into fall. It's traditionally the first harvest celebration, when the rewards of a year's worth of planting and tending are ready to reap. How have your efforts paid off? What can you clear away to make room for the future? Gather up what you've got in times of plenty, and you'll be prepared for any tougher times that come.

Mabon is the autumn equinox, when day and night are equal again. The balance of darkness and light is not only essential to magic, but also a fact of our everyday life. Transformation is in the air, and while change can be scary, it's powerful, too. What cycles do you find yourself repeating? What do you want to protect?

USING THIS LOGBOOK

Journaling strengthens your talents and helps you keep track of patterns in your life. Magic works the same way—all it takes is you.

Write down what you want to happen, and what you'll do to will it into being. Draw a sigil or symbol to anchor your intentions.

Later, return to these pages and record the effects of your spells. Observe what works and what could take another try. The reference guides in the back of this book offer an array of materials to help spice up your spells. But no need to pull out your wallet just yet—you don't need a shopping list for eye of newt and toe of frog to practice witchcraft.

Make magic in the little things. Stir your tea clockwise to draw good energy your way, and counterclockwise to banish bad vibes. Pick up that cool rock you spotted on the way home. Write an affirmation or a symbol on a scrap of paper, and put it in your pocket for good luck. Improvise, experiment, and get creative—you'll never know what works for you until you try.

Keep in mind that there are a multitude of magical traditions, old and new, from all across the world. This logbook is meant to fit your individual approach to magic and mindfulness. Some practices are culturally specific, with boundaries that ethical witches should treat with respect. It's always worthwhile to do your research so you can practice conscientiously.

IF YOU HARM NONE, DO AS YOU WILL.

YOUR BOOK OF SPELLS
INDEX

SPELL:	PAGE:	SPELL:	PAGE:

SPELL:	PAGE:	SPELL:	PAGE:

SPELL: PAGE: **SPELL:**   PAGE:

HERE'S AN EXAMPLE OF THE SPELLS PAGES THAT FOLLOW.

SPELL: *Cleansing Ritual*

Date: *6/24* 🌒🌓🌔 ⭕ 🌖🌗🌘 ⚫

Intention: *Cleanse altar, remove negative energy*

Materials: *glass jar, rainwater, selenite, moonstone, rosemary*

Elements invoked: | Fire | ✗ Water
| Earth | Air | Spirit

Actions: *Collect rainwater in a glass jar. On a full moon, close eyes and speak incantation over it, then leave in direct moonlight overnight surrounded by selenite, moonstone, and fresh rosemary.*

Incantation: *This water cleanses all it touches.*

Effects: *I've felt a bit calmer in my workspace this week, and my last spell was stronger and brought a sense of peace.*

SPELL:

Date:))))))))) ◯ ◯ ◯ ((((⬤

Intention:

Materials:

Elements invoked: ☐ Fire ☐ Water

☐ Earth ☐ Air ☐ Spirit

Actions:

Incantation:

Effects:

SPELL:

Date: 〉〉〉〉◯◯◯◯◯◯●

Intention:

Materials:

Elements invoked: ▢ **Fire**   ▢ **Water**
                       ▢ **Earth**   ▢ **Air**   ▢ **Spirit**

Actions:

Incantation:

Effects:

SPELL:

Date:

Intention:

Materials:

Elements invoked: ☐ Fire ☐ Water ☐ Earth ☐ Air ☐ Spirit

Actions:

Incantation:

Effects:

SPELL:

Date:)))))) OOO (((((●

Intention:

Materials:

Elements invoked:

	Fire		Water
	Earth		Air		Spirit

Actions:

Incantation:

Effects:

SPELL:

Date:))))) ◯◯◯((((●

Intention:

Materials:

Elements invoked: ☐ **Fire** ☐ **Water**

☐ **Earth** ☐ **Air** ☐ **Spirit**

Actions:

Incantation:

Effects:

19

SPELL:

Date:))))) ⌒ ○ ○ ⌒ (((((●

Intention:

Materials:

Elements invoked: ▢ **Fire**   ▢ **Water**

   ▢ **Earth**   ▢ **Air**   ▢ **Spirit**

Actions:

Incantation:

Effects:

SPELL:

Date:))))) ◯◯◖◖◖◖ ●

Intention:

Materials:

Elements invoked: ☐ **Fire** ☐ **Water**

☐ **Earth** ☐ **Air** ☐ **Spirit**

Actions:

Incantation:

Effects:

SPELL:

Date:))))) ◯◯◯ ((((●

Intention:

Materials:

Elements invoked: ▢ Fire ▢ Water

▢ Earth ▢ Air ▢ Spirit

Actions:

Incantation:

Effects:

SPELL:

Date:))))) ○ ○ ((((●

Intention:

Materials:

Elements invoked: ☐ Fire ☐ Water

☐ Earth ☐ Air ☐ Spirit

Actions:

Incantation:

Effects:

SPELL:

Date:))))) ◗ ◗ ○ ○ ○ ◖ ◖ ◖ ●

Intention:

Materials:

Elements invoked: ▢ **Fire** ▢ **Water**

▢ **Earth** ▢ **Air** ▢ **Spirit**

Actions:

Incantation:

Effects:

SPELL:

Date: 🌒🌒🌒🌒🌑🌑🌓🌓🌔🌔 ●

Intention:

Materials:

Elements invoked: ☐ Fire ☐ Water

☐ Earth ☐ Air ☐ Spirit

Actions:

Incantation:

Effects:

SPELL:

Date:))))))) ◯ ◯ ◯ ◯ ◯ ◯ ◯ ●

Intention:

Materials:

Elements invoked: ▢ Fire   ▢ Water

▢ Earth   ▢ Air   ▢ Spirit

Actions:

Incantation:

Effects:

SPELL:

Date:))))) ○○○ ((((●

Intention:

Materials:

Elements invoked: ▢ **Fire** ▢ **Water**

▢ **Earth** ▢ **Air** ▢ **Spirit**

Actions:

Incantation:

Effects:

SPELL:

Date:))))) ◯◯◯ ((((●

Intention:

Materials:

Elements invoked: ☐ Fire ☐ Water

☐ Earth ☐ Air ☐ Spirit

Actions:

Incantation:

Effects:

SPELL:

Date:))))) ◑ ○ ○ ◐ (((●

Intention:

Materials:

Elements invoked: ▢ Fire ▢ Water

▢ Earth ▢ Air ▢ Spirit

Actions:

Incantation:

Effects:

SPELL:

Date:)))))) ((((●

Intention:

Materials:

Elements invoked: ▢ Fire   ▢ Water

▢ Earth   ▢ Air   ▢ Spirit

Actions:

Incantation:

Effects:

SPELL:

Date:))))) ⊃ ○ ○ ((((●

Intention:

Materials:

Elements invoked: ☐ Fire ☐ Water

☐ Earth ☐ Air ☐ Spirit

Actions:

Incantation:

Effects:

SPELL:

Date:))))))) ◯ ◯ ◖ ◖ ◖ ◖ ●

Intention:

Materials:

Elements invoked: ▢ Fire ▢ Water

▢ Earth ▢ Air ▢ Spirit

Actions:

Incantation:

Effects:

SPELL:

Date:))))) ◯◯ ((((●

Intention:

Materials:

Elements invoked: ▢ Fire ▢ Water

▢ Earth ▢ Air ▢ Spirit

Actions:

Incantation:

Effects:

SPELL:

Date:)))) ◐ ○ ◐ ((((●

Intention:

Materials:

Elements invoked: ▢ Fire ▢ Water

▢ Earth ▢ Air ▢ Spirit

Actions:

Incantation:

Effects:

SPELL:

Date:))))) ⊃ ◯ ◯ ◯ ((((((●

Intention:

Materials:

Elements invoked: ▢ **Fire** ▢ **Water**

▢ **Earth** ▢ **Air** ▢ **Spirit**

Actions:

Incantation:

Effects:

SPELL:

Date:

Intention:

Materials:

Elements invoked:

	Fire		Water
Earth		Air		Spirit

Actions:

Incantation:

Effects:

SPELL:

Date:)))))) ◯ ◯ ((((●

Intention:

Materials:

Elements invoked: ▢ **Fire** ▢ **Water**

▢ **Earth** ▢ **Air** ▢ **Spirit**

Actions:

Incantation:

Effects:

SPELL:

Date:))))) OOO ((((●

Intention:

Materials:

Elements invoked: ▢ Fire ▢ Water

▢ Earth ▢ Air ▢ Spirit

Actions:

Incantation:

Effects:

SPELL:

Date:

Intention:

Materials:

Elements invoked: ☐ **Fire** ☐ **Water** ☐ **Earth** ☐ **Air** ☐ **Spirit**

Actions:

Incantation:

Effects:

SPELL:

Date:

Intention:

Materials:

Elements invoked: ☐ Fire ☐ Water

☐ Earth ☐ Air ☐ Spirit

Actions:

Incantation:

Effects:

SPELL:

Date:)))))))) ○ ○ ○ ((((●

Intention:

Materials:

Elements invoked: ☐ **Fire** ☐ **Water**

☐ **Earth** ☐ **Air** ☐ **Spirit**

Actions:

Incantation:

Effects:

SPELL:

Date:))))) ◑ ○ ○ ◐ (((●

Intention:

Materials:

Elements invoked: ☐ **Fire** ☐ **Water**
☐ **Earth** ☐ **Air** ☐ **Spirit**

Actions:

Incantation:

Effects:

SPELL:

Date:))))) ◯ ◯ ◯ (((((●

Intention:

Materials:

Elements invoked: ☐ Fire ☐ Water

☐ Earth ☐ Air ☐ Spirit

Actions:

Incantation:

Effects:

43

SPELL:

Date:))))) ◡ ◡ ◡ ◡ ◡ ◡ ●

Intention:

Materials:

Elements invoked: ☐ Fire ☐ Water

☐ Earth ☐ Air ☐ Spirit

Actions:

Incantation:

Effects:

SPELL:

Date:))))) ○ ○ ○ ((((●

Intention:

Materials:

Elements invoked: ▢ Fire   ▢ Water

▢ Earth   ▢ Air   ▢ Spirit

Actions:

Incantation:

Effects:

45

SPELL:

Date:)))))))) ((((●

Intention:

Materials:

Elements invoked: ☐ Fire   ☐ Water
                        ☐ Earth   ☐ Air   ☐ Spirit

Actions:

Incantation:

Effects:

SPELL:

Date:))))))) ◯ ◯ ◯ (((((●

Intention:

Materials:

Elements invoked: ☐ **Fire** ☐ **Water**

☐ **Earth** ☐ **Air** ☐ **Spirit**

Actions:

Incantation:

Effects:

SPELL:

Date:))))))) ◯◯◯ (((((●

Intention:

Materials:

Elements invoked: ⬜ Fire ⬜ Water

⬜ Earth ⬜ Air ⬜ Spirit

Actions:

Incantation:

Effects:

SPELL:

Date:))))))) ◯◯◯ (((((●

Intention:

Materials:

Elements invoked: ▢ **Fire** ▢ **Water**

▢ **Earth** ▢ **Air** ▢ **Spirit**

Actions:

Incantation:

Effects:

SPELL: ....

Date:)))) ◗ ◖ ○ ◐ ◑ ◕ ((((●

Intention: ....

Materials: ....

....

Elements invoked: ☐ **Fire** ☐ **Water**

☐ **Earth** ☐ **Air** ☐ **Spirit**

Actions: ....

....

....

....

....

Incantation: ....

Effects: ....

....

....

50

SPELL:

Date:)))))) ◯ ◯ ((((●

Intention:

Materials:

Elements invoked: ☐ Fire ☐ Water

☐ Earth ☐ Air ☐ Spirit

Actions:

Incantation:

Effects:

SPELL:

Date:))))) ○○○ ((((●

Intention:

Materials:

Elements invoked: ☐ **Fire** ☐ **Water**

☐ **Earth** ☐ **Air** ☐ **Spirit**

Actions:

Incantation:

Effects:

SPELL:

Date:))))) ⊃ ○ ○ ⊂ ((((●

Intention:

Materials:

Elements invoked: ▢ Fire ▢ Water

▢ Earth ▢ Air ▢ Spirit

Actions:

Incantation:

Effects:

SPELL:

Date:))))) ◯ ◯ ◯ ◯ ((((●

Intention:

Materials:

Elements invoked: ▢ Fire ▢ Water

▢ Earth ▢ Air ▢ Spirit

Actions:

Incantation:

Effects:

SPELL:

Date:))))) ○○○ ((((●

Intention:

Materials:

Elements invoked: ☐ Fire ☐ Water
☐ Earth ☐ Air ☐ Spirit

Actions:

Incantation:

Effects:

SPELL:

Date:))))) ◯◯ ((((●

Intention:

Materials:

Elements invoked: ☐ **Fire** ☐ **Water**

☐ **Earth** ☐ **Air** ☐ **Spirit**

Actions:

Incantation:

Effects:

SPELL:

Date:))))) ○○ ((((●

Intention:

Materials:

Elements invoked: ☐ Fire ☐ Water

☐ Earth ☐ Air ☐ Spirit

Actions:

Incantation:

Effects:

SPELL:

Date:)))))◯◯((((●

Intention:

Materials:

Elements invoked: ☐ Fire ☐ Water
☐ Earth ☐ Air ☐ Spirit

Actions:

Incantation:

Effects:

SPELL:

Date:

Intention:

Materials:

Elements invoked: ☐ **Fire** ☐ **Water**

☐ **Earth** ☐ **Air** ☐ **Spirit**

Actions:

Incantation:

Effects:

SPELL:

Date:))))) ○○○ ((((●

Intention:

Materials:

Elements invoked: ☐ Fire ☐ Water
☐ Earth ☐ Air ☐ Spirit

Actions:

Incantation:

Effects:

SPELL:

Date:))))) ○○○ (((●

Intention:

Materials:

Elements invoked: Fire   Water

          Earth   Air   Spirit

Actions:

Incantation:

Effects:

SPELL:

Date:))))) ⊃ ○ ○ ((((●

Intention:

Materials:

Elements invoked: ☐ Fire ☐ Water

☐ Earth ☐ Air ☐ Spirit

Actions:

Incantation:

Effects:

SPELL:

Date:))))) ◯ ◯ ◯ ((((●

Intention:

Materials:

Elements invoked: ☐ Fire   ☐ Water

☐ Earth   ☐ Air   ☐ Spirit

Actions:

Incantation:

Effects:

SPELL: ....

Date:)))))○○((((●

Intention: ....

Materials: ....

....

Elements invoked: ☐ **Fire** ☐ **Water**

☐ **Earth** ☐ **Air** ☐ **Spirit**

Actions: ....

....

....

....

Incantation: ....

Effects: ....

....

....

SPELL:

Date:))))) ⊃ ◯ ◯ ◯ ◯ ((((●

Intention:

Materials:

Elements invoked: ▢ **Fire** ▢ **Water**

▢ **Earth** ▢ **Air** ▢ **Spirit**

Actions:

Incantation:

Effects:

SPELL:

Date:)))) ◡ ◡ ◯ ◯ ◖ ◖ ◖ ◖ ●

Intention:

Materials:

Elements invoked: ▢ **Fire** ▢ **Water**

▢ **Earth** ▢ **Air** ▢ **Spirit**

Actions:

Incantation:

Effects:

SPELL:

Date:))))) ◌ ◯ ◯ ((((●

Intention:

Materials:

Elements invoked: ▢ **Fire** ▢ **Water**

▢ **Earth** ▢ **Air** ▢ **Spirit**

Actions:

Incantation:

Effects:

SPELL:

Date:))))) ◯◯◯ (((((●

Intention:

Materials:

Elements invoked: ▢ Fire ▢ Water

▢ Earth ▢ Air ▢ Spirit

Actions:

Incantation:

Effects:

SPELL:

Date:))))) ◗ ◗ ◯ ◯ ◯ ((((●

Intention:

Materials:

Elements invoked: ☐ Fire ☐ Water

☐ Earth ☐ Air ☐ Spirit

Actions:

Incantation:

Effects:

SPELL:

Date:))))) ◗ ○ ○ ◖ ◖◖◖ ●

Intention:

Materials:

Elements invoked: ▢ Fire ▢ Water

▢ Earth ▢ Air ▢ Spirit

Actions:

Incantation:

Effects:

SPELL:

Date:))))) ◯ ◯ ◯ ((((●

Intention:

Materials:

Elements invoked: ☐ Fire ☐ Water
☐ Earth ☐ Air ☐ Spirit

Actions:

Incantation:

Effects:

SPELL:

Date:))))))) ○ ○ ○ (((((⬤

Intention:

Materials:

Elements invoked: ☐ Fire ☐ Water

☐ Earth ☐ Air ☐ Spirit

Actions:

Incantation:

Effects:

SPELL:

Date:))))) ⌒ ◯ ◯ ⌒ (((((●

Intention:

Materials:

Elements invoked: ▢ **Fire** ▢ **Water**

▢ **Earth** ▢ **Air** ▢ **Spirit**

Actions:

Incantation:

Effects:

SPELL:

Date:)))))○○○((((●

Intention:

Materials:

Elements invoked: ☐ Fire ☐ Water
☐ Earth ☐ Air ☐ Spirit

Actions:

Incantation:

Effects:

SPELL:

Date:)))))) ◗ ◯ ◯ ((((●

Intention:

Materials:

Elements invoked: ☐ **Fire** ☐ **Water**

☐ **Earth** ☐ **Air** ☐ **Spirit**

Actions:

Incantation:

Effects:

SPELL:

Date:

Intention:

Materials:

Elements invoked: ☐ **Fire** ☐ **Water**

☐ **Earth** ☐ **Air** ☐ **Spirit**

Actions:

Incantation:

Effects:

SPELL:

Date: 🌙🌙🌙🌙🌗🌕🌖🌘🌒🌑🌕

Intention:

Materials:

Elements invoked: ▢ Fire ▢ Water

▢ Earth ▢ Air ▢ Spirit

Actions:

Incantation:

Effects:

SPELL:

Date:))))) ◯◯◯◯ ((((●

Intention:

Materials:

Elements invoked: ▢ **Fire**   ▢ **Water**

▢ **Earth**   ▢ **Air**   ▢ **Spirit**

Actions:

Incantation:

Effects:

SPELL:

Date:))))) ◯◯◯ ((((●

Intention:

Materials:

Elements invoked: ⬜ Fire ⬜ Water

⬜ Earth ⬜ Air ⬜ Spirit

Actions:

Incantation:

Effects:

SPELL:

Date:))))) ◯◯◯ ((((●

Intention:

Materials:

Elements invoked: ☐ Fire ☐ Water ☐ Earth ☐ Air ☐ Spirit

Actions:

Incantation:

Effects:

SPELL:

Date:)))))))) ◗ ◯ ◯ ◯ ((((((●

Intention:

Materials:

Elements invoked: ▨ **Fire** ▨ **Water**

▨ **Earth** ▨ **Air** ▨ **Spirit**

Actions:

Incantation:

Effects:

SPELL:

Date:)))))))) ◯◯◯ ((((●

Intention:

Materials:

Elements invoked: ▢ Fire ▢ Water

▢ Earth ▢ Air ▢ Spirit

Actions:

Incantation:

Effects:

SPELL:

Date:))))OOCCCC●

Intention:

Materials:

Elements invoked: ☐ Fire ☐ Water

☐ Earth ☐ Air ☐ Spirit

Actions:

Incantation:

Effects:

SPELL:

Date:))))) ◗ ◗ ◯ ◯ ◯ ((((●

Intention:

Materials:

Elements invoked: ☐ Fire ☐ Water

☐ Earth ☐ Air ☐ Spirit

Actions:

Incantation:

Effects:

SPELL:

Date:

Intention:

Materials:

Elements invoked: ☐ Fire ☐ Water

☐ Earth ☐ Air ☐ Spirit

Actions:

Incantation:

Effects:

85

SPELL:

Date:

Intention:

Materials:

Elements invoked: ☐ Fire ☐ Water

☐ Earth ☐ Air ☐ Spirit

Actions:

Incantation:

Effects:

SPELL:

Date:))))) ◯◯◯ ((((●

Intention:

Materials:

Elements invoked: ☐ **Fire** ☐ **Water**
☐ **Earth** ☐ **Air** ☐ **Spirit**

Actions:

Incantation:

Effects:

SPELL:

Date:)))))))) ◯◯◯ ◯◯ ◯◯◯◯ ●

Intention:

Materials:

Elements invoked: ☐ **Fire** ☐ **Water**

☐ **Earth** ☐ **Air** ☐ **Spirit**

Actions:

Incantation:

Effects:

SPELL:

Date:)))))) ◗ ◖ ○ ○ ((((●

Intention:

Materials:

Elements invoked: ▢ Fire ▢ Water

▢ Earth ▢ Air ▢ Spirit

Actions:

Incantation:

Effects:

SPELL:

Date:))))) ○○○ ((((●

Intention:

Materials:

Elements invoked: ▢ **Fire** ▢ **Water**

▢ **Earth** ▢ **Air** ▢ **Spirit**

Actions:

Incantation:

Effects:

SPELL:

Date:))))) ◯◯◯ ((((●

Intention:

Materials:

Elements invoked: ▢ Fire   ▢ Water

▢ Earth   ▢ Air   ▢ Spirit

Actions:

Incantation:

Effects:

SPELL:

Date:)))))◯◯(((((●

Intention:

Materials:

Elements invoked: ☐ Fire ☐ Water
☐ Earth ☐ Air ☐ Spirit

Actions:

Incantation:

Effects:

SPELL:

Date:

Intention:

Materials:

Elements invoked: ▢ Fire   ▢ Water

▢ Earth   ▢ Air   ▢ Spirit

Actions:

Incantation:

Effects:

SPELL:

Date:))))) ◯ ◯ ◯ ((((●

Intention:

Materials:

Elements invoked: ▢ **Fire**   ▢ **Water**
                         ▢ **Earth**   ▢ **Air**   ▢ **Spirit**

Actions:

Incantation:

Effects:

SPELL:

Date:)))))))) ((((((●

Intention:

Materials:

Elements invoked: ▢ Fire ▢ Water

▢ Earth ▢ Air ▢ Spirit

Actions:

Incantation:

Effects:

SPELL:

Date:

Intention:

Materials:

Elements invoked: ☐ Fire ☐ Water

☐ Earth ☐ Air ☐ Spirit

Actions:

Incantation:

Effects:

SPELL:

Date:

Intention:

Materials:

Elements invoked: Fire Water

Earth Air Spirit

Actions:

Incantation:

Effects:

SPELL:

Date:))))) ◯ ◯ ◯ ◯ ((((●

Intention:

Materials:

Elements invoked: ☐ **Fire** ☐ **Water**

☐ **Earth** ☐ **Air** ☐ **Spirit**

Actions:

Incantation:

Effects:

SPELL:

Date:)))) ( )) ((((((●

Intention:

Materials:

Elements invoked: ▢ Fire ▢ Water
▢ Earth ▢ Air ▢ Spirit

Actions:

Incantation:

Effects:

SPELL:

Date:

Intention:

Materials:

Elements invoked: ☐ Fire   ☐ Water

☐ Earth   ☐ Air   ☐ Spirit

Actions:

Incantation:

Effects:

SPELL:

Date:

Intention:

Materials:

Elements invoked: Fire   Water

   Earth   Air   Spirit

Actions:

Incantation:

Effects:

SPELL:

Date:)))) ⊃ ○ ○ ((((●

Intention:

Materials:

Elements invoked: ⬜ Fire   ⬜ Water

⬜ Earth   ⬜ Air   ⬜ Spirit

Actions:

Incantation:

Effects:

SPELL:

Date:))))) ○ ○ ((((●

Intention:

Materials:

Elements invoked: ☐ **Fire** ☐ **Water**

☐ **Earth** ☐ **Air** ☐ **Spirit**

Actions:

Incantation:

Effects:

SPELL:

Date: ☽ ☽ ☽ ◔ ○ ○ ◖ ◖ ◖ ◖ ●

Intention:

Materials:

Elements invoked: ☐ **Fire**   ☐ **Water**

☐ **Earth**   ☐ **Air**   ☐ **Spirit**

Actions:

Incantation:

Effects:

SPELL:

Date:))))) ◯◯◯ ((((●

Intention:

Materials:

Elements invoked: ▢ **Fire** ▢ **Water**

▢ **Earth** ▢ **Air** ▢ **Spirit**

Actions:

Incantation:

Effects:

SPELL:

Date:)))) ○○○ ((((●

Intention:

Materials:

Elements invoked: ☐ Fire ☐ Water
☐ Earth ☐ Air ☐ Spirit

Actions:

Incantation:

Effects:

SPELL:

Date:

Intention:

Materials:

Elements invoked: Fire Water

Earth Air Spirit

Actions:

Incantation:

Effects:

SPELL:

Date:

Intention:

Materials:

Elements invoked: ☐ Fire ☐ Water

☐ Earth ☐ Air ☐ Spirit

Actions:

Incantation:

Effects:

SPELL:

Date:

Intention:

Materials:

Elements invoked: ☐ Fire   ☐ Water

☐ Earth   ☐ Air   ☐ Spirit

Actions:

Incantation:

Effects:

SPELL:

Date:)))))))))) O O O ((((●

Intention:

Materials:

Elements invoked: ☐ Fire ☐ Water
☐ Earth ☐ Air ☐ Spirit

Actions:

Incantation:

Effects:

SPELL:

Date:

Intention:

Materials:

Elements invoked:
☐ Fire ☐ Water
☐ Earth ☐ Air ☐ Spirit

Actions:

Incantation:

Effects:

SPELL:

Date:)))))) ◯ ◯ ◯ (((((●

Intention:

Materials:

Elements invoked: ☐ **Fire** ☐ **Water** ☐ **Earth** ☐ **Air** ☐ **Spirit**

Actions:

Incantation:

Effects:

SPELL:

Date:))))) ⏾ ○ ○ ◐ ◑ ◖◗ ●

Intention:

Materials:

Elements invoked: ☐ Fire ☐ Water
☐ Earth ☐ Air ☐ Spirit

Actions:

Incantation:

Effects:

SPELL:

Date:

Intention:

Materials:

Elements invoked: ☐ Fire ☐ Water

☐ Earth ☐ Air ☐ Spirit

Actions:

Incantation:

Effects:

SPELL:

Date:))))) ○ ○ (((((●

Intention:

Materials:

Elements invoked: ▢ Fire ▢ Water
                        ▢ Earth ▢ Air ▢ Spirit

Actions:

Incantation:

Effects:

SPELL:

Date: 〗〗〗〗〗 ◔ ○ ○ ◖ ◖ ◖◖ ●

Intention:

Materials:

Elements invoked: ▢ **Fire** ▢ **Water**

▢ **Earth** ▢ **Air** ▢ **Spirit**

Actions:

Incantation:

Effects:

SPELL:

Date:))))) ○○○ ((((●

Intention:

Materials:

Elements invoked: ▢ **Fire** ▢ **Water**

▢ **Earth** ▢ **Air** ▢ **Spirit**

Actions:

Incantation:

Effects:

SPELL:

Date:))))) ◯ ◯ ◯ ((((●

Intention:

Materials:

Elements invoked: ☐ Fire ☐ Water

☐ Earth ☐ Air ☐ Spirit

Actions:

Incantation:

Effects:

SPELL:

Date:

Intention:

Materials:

Elements invoked: Fire   Water

      Earth   Air   Spirit

Actions:

Incantation:

Effects:

SPELL:

Date:))))))))))))) (((((●

Intention:

Materials:

Elements invoked: ☐ Fire   ☐ Water

☐ Earth   ☐ Air   ☐ Spirit

Actions:

Incantation:

Effects:

SPELL:

Date:))))) OOO ((((●

Intention:

Materials:

Elements invoked: ☐ Fire ☐ Water

☐ Earth ☐ Air ☐ Spirit

Actions:

Incantation:

Effects:

SPELL:

Date:

Intention:

Materials:

Elements invoked: ☐ Fire ☐ Water

☐ Earth ☐ Air ☐ Spirit

Actions:

Incantation:

Effects:

SPELL:

Date:))))) ◯ ◯ ◯ (((((●

Intention:

Materials:

Elements invoked: ☐ Fire ☐ Water

☐ Earth ☐ Air ☐ Spirit

Actions:

Incantation:

Effects:

SPELL:

Date: 〉〉〉〉〉〉 ◯ ◯ ◯ ◯ ◯ ◯ ◯ ◯ ◯ ●

Intention:

Materials:

Elements invoked: ☐ Fire ☐ Water
☐ Earth ☐ Air ☐ Spirit

Actions:

Incantation:

Effects:

124

SPELL:

Date:

Intention:

Materials:

Elements invoked: ⬜ **Fire** ⬜ **Water**

⬜ **Earth** ⬜ **Air** ⬜ **Spirit**

Actions:

Incantation:

Effects:

SPELL:

Date:))))) ◯ ◯ ◯ (((((●

Intention:

Materials:

Elements invoked: Fire   Water
              Earth   Air   Spirit

Actions:

Incantation:

Effects:

SPELL:

Date:

Intention:

Materials:

Elements invoked: ▢ **Fire** ▢ **Water**

▢ **Earth** ▢ **Air** ▢ **Spirit**

Actions:

Incantation:

Effects:

SPELL:

Date:))))))) ○○ ○ ((((●

Intention:

Materials:

Elements invoked: ⬜ Fire ⬜ Water
⬜ Earth ⬜ Air ⬜ Spirit

Actions:

Incantation:

Effects:

SPELL:

Date:)))))) ◯ ◯ ◯ ((((●

Intention:

Materials:

Elements invoked: ▢ **Fire** ▢ **Water**

▢ **Earth** ▢ **Air** ▢ **Spirit**

Actions:

Incantation:

Effects:

SPELL: ....

Date:))))) ○○○ ((((●

Intention: ....

Materials: ....

....

Elements invoked: ☐ **Fire**   ☐ **Water**

              ☐ **Earth**   ☐ **Air**   ☐ **Spirit**

Actions: ....

....

....

....

Incantation: ....

Effects: ....

....

....

SPELL:

Date:

Intention:

Materials:

Elements invoked:

	Fire		Water
	Earth		Air		Spirit

Actions:

Incantation:

Effects:

SPELL:

Date:)))))) ◯ ◯ ◯ ((((⬤

Intention:

Materials:

Elements invoked: ▢ **Fire** ▢ **Water**

▢ **Earth** ▢ **Air** ▢ **Spirit**

Actions:

Incantation:

Effects:

SPELL:

Date:))))))))) ◯ ◯ ((((((●

Intention:

Materials:

Elements invoked: ☐ Fire   ☐ Water
                      ☐ Earth   ☐ Air   ☐ Spirit

Actions:

Incantation:

Effects:

SPELL:

Date: ⟩⟩⟩⟩◯◯◯◯⟨⟨⟨●

Intention:

Materials:

Elements invoked: ☐ Fire ☐ Water

☐ Earth ☐ Air ☐ Spirit

Actions:

Incantation:

Effects:

SPELL:

Date:

Intention:

Materials:

Elements invoked: ☐ **Fire** ☐ **Water**

☐ **Earth** ☐ **Air** ☐ **Spirit**

Actions:

Incantation:

Effects:

SPELL:

Date:))))) ○ ○ ○ ((((●

Intention:

Materials:

Elements invoked: ▢ Fire   ▢ Water

▢ Earth   ▢ Air   ▢ Spirit

Actions:

Incantation:

Effects:

SPELL:

Date:

Intention:

Materials:

Elements invoked: ☐ Fire ☐ Water

☐ Earth ☐ Air ☐ Spirit

Actions:

Incantation:

Effects:

SPELL:

Date:)))))◯◯◯(((((●

Intention:

Materials:

Elements invoked: ▢ Fire ▢ Water
▢ Earth ▢ Air ▢ Spirit

Actions:

Incantation:

Effects:

SPELL:

Date:

Intention:

Materials:

Elements invoked: ⬜ **Fire** ⬜ **Water**

⬜ **Earth** ⬜ **Air** ⬜ **Spirit**

Actions:

Incantation:

Effects:

MATERIALS GUIDE

Although the single most important ingredient of any spell is your own will-power, physical materials can help you focus and manifest your wishes. Here's a quick guide to some common, adaptable ingredients, easy to find and use in all sorts of spells.

Note that magic is a supplement, not a substitute, for medical care. Seek medicine first if you're unwell.

HERBS AND SPICES

NAME	USES
Aloe	*beauty, relationship health, protection from accidents, calling the moon*
Basil	*prosperity, happiness, money, freedom from fear and insecurity*
Bay Leaf	*good luck, purification, closure, strength*
Chamomile	*relaxation, good dreams, breaking curses, letting go*
Cinnamon	*health, success, passion, positivity*
Cloves	*protecting friendships, banishing negative forces*
Lavender	*love, opportunity, clairvoyance, freedom from stress and anxiety*
Mint	*communication, energy, courage, overcoming obstacles*
Pine	*optimism, resilience, fresh perspective, safety*
Rosemary	*clear thinking, good memory, love, all-purpose protection and blessing*
Sage	*longevity, wisdom, protection, recovery from grief*
Salt	*absorbing energy, shielding from harm*
Star Anise	*luck, awareness, spiritual strength, extra power*
Thyme	*affection, courage, loyalty, happiness*

OILS AND INCENSE

NAME	USES
Bergamot	*stress relief, energy, optimism, success*
Jasmine	*good dreams, new ideas, wealth, spiritual love*
Patchouli	*attraction, abundance, prosperity, love*
Rose	*romance, close friendships, fertility, peace at home*
Sandalwood	*cleansing, protection, wish fulfillment, peace of mind*
Vanilla	*love and lust, restoration, vitality, good moods*

These and other "essential" oils are best used sparingly. Dilute them first with water, olive oil, or other common plant-based oils. Always use a ventilated, fire-safe space when lighting incense.

CRYSTALS

NAME	USES
Amethyst	*balance, calm, fulfillment*
Aventurine	*luck, wealth, imagination*
Carnelian	*passion, inspiration, confidence*
Citrine	*ambition, adaptability, mindfulness*
Clear Quartz	*clarity, all-purpose focus and amplification*
Garnet	*self-esteem, victory, hope*
Hematite	*grounding, concentration, inner strength*
Rose Quartz	*love, inner peace, forgiveness*
Selenite	*positivity, cleansing, unblocking*
Tourmaline	*banishing, soothing, security*

COLORS

NAME	USES
Red	*passion, attraction, desire, courage, strength*
Orange	*exuberance, creative energy, self-esteem, opportunity*
Yellow	*joy, confidence, intellectual clarity, truth*
Green	*prosperity, luck, fertility, renewal*
Blue	*tranquility, relaxation, self-improvement, health*
Purple	*power, insight, memory, emotional intelligence*
Pink	*romance, friendship, harmony, emotional health*
Brown	*grounding, endurance, generosity, finding lost things*
Black	*protection, reversal, deflecting negativity*
White	*safety, clarity, vision, enlightenment*

Color themes are often used in candle magic to emphasize the intentions of a spell. You can also play with color in your other ingredients, or even with markers and pens. When in doubt, use white; it contains all other colors and works as a blank slate.

ADD YOUR OWN MATERIALS

NAME	USES

MUSINGS